A Vision of Hope

Reflections
Andrew Drasen

A Vision of Hope Media, LLC

A Vision of Hope: Reflections

For permission requests, contact:

Andrew Drasen
Email: andrew@avisionofhopebook.com
Website: www.avisionofhopebook.com

Published by A Vision of Hope Media
Franklin, WI, USA

ISBN (Paperback): 979-8-9996415-4-0
ISBN (eBook): 979-8-9996415-3-3

Cover design by Andrew Drasen
Interior design by Andrew Drasen

Printed in the United States of America

Library of Congress Control Number: 2025920025

***

Introduction

These reflections were originally written to be included in A Vision of Hope. Like the chapters of that memoir, they were born in the same season of collapse and transformation, written from jail, recovery, relapse, and redemption. They come from the same truth.

At first, I intended to weave them into the main narrative, letting each reflection serve as a pause, a lens, a mirror. But as the manuscript grew, it became clear that the story needed room to breathe, and these reflections needed a space of their own.

So, this companion was born, A Vision of Hope: Reflections.
Not an afterthought. Not bonus content.
But a continuation of the same heartbeat, written for anyone still navigating their storm.

Use these entries however you need:
As meditations.
As journaling prompts.
As anchors.
As reminders that recovery, whether from addiction, shame, loss, or anything else, is not only possible but already underway the moment you pause long enough to reflect.

These words come from the same road.

I hope they meet you exactly where you are.
— **Andrew Drasen**

Preface

This book is the middle piece of a three-part conversation.

The memoir tells the story. Reflections pulls lessons out of that story — what I learned, what I am still learning, and where my thinking has changed. The companion Workbook turns those lessons into things you can practice. Together, they form a path: story to perspective to action.

Where I am coming from:

What follows is shaped by my lived experience: addiction, recovery, faith, family, the legal system, victories, failures, and the years I spent getting honest about all of it. I am not a guru. I am one person telling the truth as I have come to see it. If you disagree with something, good. Bring your view. I welcome opposing viewpoints and real debate done in good faith. I am still learning.

Why some entries lean political:

A few chapters wade into culture, law, policing, and policy. I wrote them because the personal and the public are connected. The point is not outrage. The point is solutions. If we cannot talk about systems, we leave people to carry everything alone. Read these chapters as proposals from one citizen, not commandments: problem, context, ideas we can test and improve together.

What this book is (and is not):

It is straight talk. Short reflections you can read in a few minutes and sit with. It is a bridge between the memoir's emotion to the workbook's action.

It is not medical, legal, or therapeutic advice. If you need professional help, get it. If you are in immediate danger, contact local emergency services.

It is not a sermon or a demand that you agree with me. Take what helps and challenge what does not.

Facts and perspectives:

Every effort has been made to ensure the examples and claims in these reflections were accurate at the time of writing. I have checked my facts, but this book is not a research paper. It is a collection of reflections rooted in lived experience. I encourage you to fact-check, explore, and verify. If something does not sound right, look it up, weigh it against other perspectives, and draw your own conclusions. That is how dialogue grows and how truth becomes stronger.

How to read this book

You have three good options:

Front to back. The reflections move from inner work to relationships and community to purpose and the bigger picture.

Dip in. Open to what you need today — Acceptance, Complacency, Recovery and Trauma, Taking Action, Purpose, Reality — and go from there.

With the Workbook. Read an entry and answer the corresponding workbook questions for practical application and growth.

"Reflection" matters only if it shapes real life. When an entry hits you, write a few lines about why. If it stings, ask what it touched. If it lights you up, ask what step it is pointing you toward. I wrote these pieces to be short on drama and long on use.

Using this with the Workbook:

If the memoir showed the storm, these reflections were written in the quiet after. The Workbook is where you roll up your sleeves. When an essay connects, turn to the matching prompts and tools and put it to work that same day. Reading changes your mind. Practice changes your life.

A note on dialogue:

We will not fix anything by shouting past each other. Here is what I am asking from you, and what I am committing to myself:

Lead with curiosity over certainty.

Disagree honestly and respectfully. Attack ideas, not people.

Keep the goal in sight: reduce harm, increase dignity, improve outcomes.

If an entry makes you want to argue with me, perfect. Argue toward something better.

Final word:

I wrote this book to name what I have seen, to own what I have done, and to offer what I can. If a page helps you move even one inch — from shame to honesty, from fear to courage, from isolation to community — then it was worth writing. Thank you for giving it your time and for bringing your voice to the table.

Let's get to work.

Part I: Foundations of Inner Change

Explores identity, healing, and the roots of transformation

"You are allowed to be both a masterpiece and a work in progress simultaneously."— *Sophia Bush*

Self-Acceptance

I like to talk about acceptance. I want to take it a step further and explore how acceptance, when misunderstood, can hold us back. It's essential that we accept ourselves as we are, flaws and all. We shouldn't hide parts of ourselves for the sake of others. If we need to do that, then those individuals don't belong in our lives in the first place and are simply taking space and time that could be occupied by someone we can be our True Selves around.

With that said, we should never use acceptance as an excuse to stop growing. If we have a particular trait that no longer benefits us, we need to look at why we hold on to it and not simply accept it as part of us.

Maybe you grew up in a rough neighborhood. As a result, you acted with hostility and aggression, lacking trust as a means for survival, so as not to become a victim. Yet, you carry that hostility into the workplace, continually losing your job because you snap at your supervisor because he 'talked to you crazy.' Or maybe you push other people away before they get too close, not willing to allow yourself to feel vulnerable, not allowing the chance for someone else to hurt you. Yet, you often feel alone as a result. Whereas the traits of aggression, hostility, and a lack of trust once served you, they are now a burden, hindering you from advancing at work (or even maintaining a job) and from developing intimate relationships.

Perhaps you grew up in an abusive household. As a result, you learned to be nice to avoid rocking the boat and making things worse for yourself. Yet, because of this, you never learned how to stand up for yourself, to be assertive, to let your wants and your needs be known, instead choosing to suffer in silence. You enter every relationship wanting to make the other person happy, all the while neglecting your happiness.

If I'm constantly late for work, family functions, literally everything, I can accept that I'm a procrastinator; that it's just part of who I am. But if it's causing things to happen that I don't want to happen, then maybe I should look at that. That's the thing. We get to choose who we are. Who we were and how we've always been doesn't have to be who we are today. We are constantly evolving, being shaped by our experiences and how we look at them.

The same is true beyond habits. It applies to our identity as well.

We don't get to choose everything about our identity. We don't get to choose who we are sexually attracted to, what we are naturally good or bad at, our mental capacity/ability to learn and retain information, or what makes us feel fulfilled as a person. In the same breath, we can choose our traits, our habits, our values, beliefs, attitudes, thoughts, and behaviors. We can change that through reflection, self-analysis, therapeutic tools, and examining whether our perception is based on reality or our perception of reality. Through developing an understanding of self, we can know who we are and embrace it.

But don't let self-acceptance become an excuse to stop growing.

It should fuel your evolution, not stall it.

Growth is a form of self-respect.

"Acceptance doesn't mean resignation; it means understanding that something is what it is and that there's got to be a way through it."— Michael J. Fox

Acceptance

Context Note:
This reflection shares my personal opinions based on lived experience. I do not claim to have all the answers. My goal is to challenge thinking, not dictate it. If you disagree, that is healthy. Opposing views help refine what works and what does not. The point is not to resolve debates but to open dialogue about how laws, systems, and beliefs shape our lives.

I want to talk about acceptance. Acceptance can be incredibly cleansing. When we learn to practice it, we begin to heal. Most of our suffering comes from resisting what is. We get depressed because we cannot accept our current situation, whether it is losing a loved one, a relationship ending, losing a job, or losing our freedom.

When I was arrested in 2014 and offered seven years in prison on top of two years of revocation, I had no choice but to practice acceptance. Acceptance did not mean giving up. It meant acknowledging the reality in front of me and focusing only on what I could control. Those first few weeks were brutal. I did not speak to my family for three weeks. But once I accepted my situation, my mind finally calmed.

Stress is the mind resisting what is. Preparing, planning, and taking action all matter, but once we have done what is in our control, the outcome will unfold regardless of how much we worry. Worry changes nothing except how we feel, and usually for the worse.

The Serenity Prayer captures this perfectly:
"God, grant me the serenity to accept the things I cannot change, the courage to change the things I can, and the wisdom to know the difference."

When we try to control people or circumstances, conflict erupts both inside and outside of us. Internally, it creates stress, anxiety, anger, resentment, and misunderstanding. Externally, it damages relationships, fuels conflict, and leads to outcomes we never intended. We can influence, but we cannot control what others think, say, or do.

You see this lack of acceptance everywhere. An abusive husband tries to control his wife and children because he cannot accept that they are separate people with their own thoughts. When they do not conform, he uses anger or violence as an attempt to force control. But we cannot control other people. To believe we can is ego.

Religion can also show this pattern. Many institutions position themselves as gate-keepers between us and our higher power. I believe divinity is something we access from within. When religious doctrine tries to dictate how others must think or live, conflict is created. Humans do not all share the same beliefs, nor should they.

The government often falls into the same trap. In my view, its role should be to guide and support, not micromanage every aspect of our lives. Laws often cross into attempting to control personal choices instead of honoring free will. Whether it is banning certain substances, restricting marriage rights, or deciding what adults can do with their bodies, too many laws try to enforce morality instead of promoting informed decision-making. I believe many of these laws violate both the human spirit and personal sovereignty.

This is not anti-government. The government provides necessary services. But I believe our system has drifted far from its intended purpose. The political process has become a performance designed to maintain power, not elevate truth. Enormous sums of money fuel elections that could instead fund schools, healthcare, or infra-structure. Voting restrictions silence voices that deserve to be heard. The two-party system encourages conformity instead of genuine leadership.

I accept that the system is broken, but I also believe in doing what I can to help fix it. That begins with understanding what we can control and what we cannot.

So, I return to the words that brought me peace when I had none:

"God, grant me the serenity to accept the things I cannot change, the courage to change the things I can, and the wisdom to know the difference."

"Worry does not empty tomorrow of its sorrow, it empties today of its strength."— Corrie ten Boom

Faith and Anxiety

Living with faith is a much easier, more peaceful, less taxing, and less stressful way to live. To have that inherent belief, that trust that everything will work out. To not question or try to control everything and everyone. And to recognize what we cannot control, and to let go of our vain attempts to dictate situations, people, or outcomes.

With faith comes a belief that what we go through, we are strong enough to endure. What does not kill us makes us stronger. The only time this fails is when we allow our circumstances to determine our happiness. Those of us who let circumstances dictate our emotional state end up crippled by situations through no fault of their own, other than their lack of faith. It is so much easier to enjoy the ride when we are not anxious over the next turn or lamenting the previous one. If we live in yesterday or fret over tomorrow, we end up wasting today.

I feel that anxiety is worrying over something that has yet to happen. It is a projection of our fears. It is impossible to have faith and be afraid at the same time. Being anxious serves no purpose.

Whether it is something extreme like running with the bulls, something every day like worrying about what people think, or something high stakes like probation, anxiety plays the same role: it robs us of peace.

There is a difference between physical sensation and anxiety. If you are running with the bulls in Barcelona, you will feel physical sensations: increased blood pressure, quicker pulse, adrenaline. That is your fight or flight response in full effect. This does not necessarily mean you are anxious. Anxiety is more of a mental preoccupation. While it can lead to physical sensations, they are not the same.

In the Barcelona example, it would not help to be preoccupied with the fear of being gored by a bull. By obsessing over that fear, we become less aware of our surroundings, which makes the feared outcome more likely, not less. With a clear mind, we are heightened by the adrenaline already coursing through us. We are more in tune and less distracted. Maybe we feel that bull creeping up on us and adjust accordingly, while if we were anxious, we would have missed the subtle cues. Maybe we hear a bull to our right, just outside our peripherals, that we would not have heard if we were busy spiraling in fear. Anxiety hinders decision-making because it preoccupies the mind instead of connecting us with the environment.

This is an extreme example, but even in ordinary life, anxiety limits us. It takes away our presence of mind and traps us in projected fears instead of connecting us to what is actually happening around us. Anxiety affects our interactions, our surroundings, our focus, and our peace. It multiplies pain instead of preventing it.

I know anxiety well. I suffered from social anxiety and feared how others would view me. This caused me to avoid interactions I genuinely wanted because I worried about how they would go. What if I said something stupid? What if they did not like me? What if, what if, what if. My fears were almost always exaggerated. Even if I said something dumb, so what? We have all said something we immediately regretted. Usually, we hold onto that feeling long after everyone else has forgotten about it. Anxiety makes it bigger than it is and increases the chance we repeat the same mistake because we are stuck in our heads instead of being present.

Then there was the anxiety I felt when using drugs while on probation, knowing I was dirty and wondering if the clean urine I had would be the right temperature. I spent days wondering if I would be clean by the time I saw my probation agent. I spent hours researching how long drugs stay in your system, or remedies to flush them out. What will be, will be. At that point, stressing afterwards was pointless. All of it could have been avoided had I made different decisions, but the point is this: worrying did nothing to change the outcome. All it did was steal my peace in the days leading up to it.

Anxiety is the fear of something that has not yet happened. Many times, the potential consequences are exaggerated, but even when they are not, anxiety is still not beneficial. The next time you are anxious, I challenge you to let it go. Be prepared, do what you can, and have faith that everything will turn out as it should. Do not let anxiety rob you of your peace.

Let faith carry what fear cannot.

"Depression is the inability to construct a future."— Rollo May

Depression

Depression is heavy. It can leave us feeling hopeless, as if there is no way out of our current situation. It is emotionally and physically taxing, draining us of joy.

I have known depression. One of my first attempts to get clean at 19, I remember sitting on my bed at my parents' house, scrolling through my phone and seeing no one I could call who would be good for me. I remember thinking, "Is this it? I am 19 years old, have no healthy friends, and nothing to do on a Friday night." I broke down in tears and went to sleep by 8:00 p.m. I mourned the loss of the only coping skill I had ever trusted. Drugs had been my best friend, the one I turned to for everything. Without them, I felt empty. I wondered if this was what the rest of my life would look like.

Later, I learned that part of what I felt was post-acute withdrawal syndrome, or PAWS. Even after the physical withdrawals end, the brain can take months or years to recalibrate. But at the time, all I knew was hopelessness.

Many of us try to drown our sorrows in a bottle, a pill, or a drug, but this often makes things worse. We push feelings down only for them to come back stronger. I watched my mom go through this for years. Depression swallowed her whole. She numbed herself with liquor and mindless television. She was grieving over her relationship with my father, my struggles, her distance from my sister, losing her job, and losing her sense of purpose. She stopped calling friends and stopped answering when they called. Isolation became her default. Things did not change until she chose to change them.

The first step is taking an honest look at our situation, acknowledging any role we played in it, and accepting what is so we can move forward. Depression often comes from mourning what was instead of focusing on what is. We grieve the loss of a loved one, a job, a relationship, or a version of our life that no longer exists. We cling to what used to be, which pulls us out of the present and strips us of peace.

We stop finding joy in the things that once made us feel alive. We feel numb. We lose our identity. Acceptance is the doorway back.

What helped me was practicing acceptance. I came to understand that change is the only constant in life. Fighting it only creates suffering. We cannot control most of what happens to us, but we can always choose how we respond.

There are cases of clinical depression caused by a chemical imbalance, and medication can be necessary. There is no shame in that. It may take trial and error, so it is important to monitor symptoms, take the medication consistently, and communicate honestly with your care team. Needing medication does not mean weakness. Your brain deserves the same care as any other organ.

There is also situational depression, which is tied to life circumstances. This can be addressed through therapy, meditation, physical activity, challenging our thoughts, building a routine, and intentionally engaging in activities that bring pleasure or curiosity.

What matters most is that we keep moving, even when it feels impossible. Depression is heavy, but it is not final. With faith, acceptance, and action, we can climb out. The battle is within — choose victory.

"Forgiveness is unlocking the door to set someone free and realizing you were the prisoner."— Max Lucado

Forgiveness

Forgiveness is a tough nut to crack. It is easy in concept, but hard in practice, especially when it involves the people closest to us. Strangers usually are not close enough to us to require meaningful forgiveness (outside of extreme cases). Yes, sometimes we may need to forgive a stranger responsible for a crime, a loss, or harm. But generally, we are not attached enough to strangers for them to impact us deeply. How hard is it to forgive someone who cut us off in traffic, was rude, or took a parking spot? Annoying, sure, but if you cannot let that go, that is more of a sign that anger management is needed than a test of forgiveness.

The people we struggle to forgive are usually those who have breached our trust or failed to meet our expectations. Many of us hold onto anger or resentment out of pride. *I cannot believe she cheated on me. I cannot believe he stole from me. How dare they talk to me that way!* We think that forgiving someone means they "get away with it." But forgiveness does not mean what happened was OK. It does not excuse the behavior. It does not require letting the person back into your life. Forgiveness does not let them off the hook, but it lets **you** off the chain.

To me, forgiveness is about moving on. It is letting go of the negative feelings to allow the memory to stop hurting you over and over again. By practicing forgiveness, we take back power and control over our thoughts, feelings, and emotions.

The hardest person for me to forgive was Jana. Every time I thought about her or Trevor, I became enraged just hearing their names. I would be brought right back to the moment I was wronged, reliving the betrayal in my mind as if it were happening again. I would feel the anger wash over me without either of them even being in the room. She failed to live up to the standards I hold for myself and the people around me. I was hurt, and I kept reliving the pain by refusing to forgive.

Her actions stayed alive inside me long after she was gone from my life. Eventually, I learned to forgive her. I did so not for her benefit, because she would never again have a place in my life. I forgave her so I could leave what happened in the past and stop letting it dictate how I felt in the present or how I would feel in the future. By forgiving, I did not say I was OK with what she did. I said I was done letting it control me.

There is real healing power in forgiveness. Letting go of negativity is incredibly cleansing. We will all be wronged by someone we care about at some point. What happens afterward is up to us. We can hang onto the anger, hurt, resentment, and betrayal until they stack like Tetris pieces, building a wall that leaves us bitter, disconnected, and alone. Or we can choose to forgive, release the pain, and move on from the ghosts that keep haunting us.

Forgiveness has nothing to do with the other person, yet it has everything to do with us. We do not need to carry the weight of the world. We can choose to set it down and move on.

"Trauma creates change you don't choose. Healing is about creating change you do choose."— Michelle Rosenthal

Recovery/Trauma

Recovery to me is not just about addiction. We are all recovering from something: childhood abuse or neglect, bullying, sexual assault, mental or physical illness, a failed relationship, the loss of someone important, or the death of a loved one. Sometimes it is the loss of a dream or a vision we once had for our lives. Sometimes it is our self-esteem or sense of worth. No matter what, every one of us is recovering from something.

We are all silent warriors trying to overcome, trying to make the best of our lives despite the events that shaped us. Past trauma is insidious. It affects our belief system, our thoughts, our feelings, and our behaviors. Some effects are obvious. Others require digging to understand why we think as we think, feel as we feel, and behave as we do.

Take my own example. I shared how I was bullied when I was young. That experience shaped the core belief that outward appearance determined worth. That success was what others could see. That other people got to decide who I was. Without their approval, I felt less than.

Those beliefs created thoughts like:
"No one likes me because I'm fat."
"Fat people are less important."
"I have to be perfect at everything else to make up for this."

Those thoughts produced feelings of inadequacy, rejection, and failure. That led to behaviors: people pleasing, doing whatever I could to make others accept me. How could I accept myself if they didn't?

There were positives. I got good grades. I developed humor to fit in. I played sports and karate for belonging. But there were negatives too. I was timid. I avoided talking to girls because I assumed they would reject me. I never shared what hurt me because I didn't want anyone to see weakness. I agreed to things I didn't want to do out of fear of disappointing others and confirming I was a failure.

As I got older, the same core belief, that I needed others' approval to feel worthy, just evolved. My thoughts became:
"Others are better than me, so I need to stand out."

"If I act fearless, people won't know I'm afraid."
"If I have more than others, they'll see I have value."

Those thoughts produced feelings of doubt masked as confidence, fear of rejection masked as bravado, and anxiety hidden behind risk-taking. Those feelings led to self-destructive behaviors: using and selling drugs, acting like school didn't matter, breaking my parents' trust, and caring more about peer approval than my own values.

Beliefs lead to thoughts, thoughts lead to feelings, feelings lead to behaviors.

Our belief system often comes from what we have been through. It comes from our family, our environment, society, traumatic experiences, and painful relationships. We talk to ourselves more than we talk to anyone else. It matters what we are telling ourselves. We should examine whether our beliefs reflect reality or only our perception of it.

If we believe we've been wronged, we will feel anger. If we believe we are powerless, we will feel hopeless. But if we reframe how we think, we can change how we feel and how we act.

Trauma shapes beliefs in different ways. Maybe we were victims of a hate crime and developed distrust of an entire group. Maybe a family member was murdered, and we concluded that all criminals are evil. Maybe a partner cheated, and now every future partner is assumed guilty until proven innocent.

We do not have to stay stuck in beliefs that no longer serve us. We can challenge them. We can change the lens. We can assign new meaning, with an open mind, and break the pattern.

What if instead of mistrusting an entire group after a hate crime, we chose to learn, bridge gaps, and work toward unity? What if healing led us to help others heal, to raise awareness, to build understanding rather than resentment?

What if instead of coldness toward criminals, we turn tragedy into purpose: forming support groups, participating in restorative justice, helping perpetrators understand the impact of their actions, and finding our own healing through helping others?

What if instead of carrying mistrust from a partner's betrayal into every new relationship, we paused, reflected, and grew? Maybe examine our own role. Maybe we were neglectful, took them for granted, or failed to communicate effectively. Maybe we become whole again before stepping into something new, creating a more interdependent and meaningful partnership.

My point is simple: we all have trauma. We all have work to do. People hurt us. Things happen that we did not choose. And things we want sometimes do not happen.

But we owe it to ourselves to look at our past honestly and talk about it. We are only as sick as our secrets. Secrets lose their power when brought to light.

Just because something bad was done to you does not mean it defines who you are. These events are things that happened. Nothing more. Nothing less. They do not determine your worth unless you give them that power.

Be fearless. Examine your past. Challenge the thoughts that keep you stuck. Let go.

Accept your past so it no longer dictates your present or determines your future.

You are not your trauma. You are your transformation.

Allow yourself to heal and move on.

You will be glad you did.

Part II: Rebuilding Perspective

Challenges perception, reframes experience, and introduces spiritual concepts

"Ethics is knowing the difference between what you have a right to do and what is right to do."— Potter Stewart

Ethics

It is easy to be ethical when life is easy. When everything is smooth, money is flowing, the family is smiling, and nothing is shaking the boat, everyone loves to talk about their integrity. But true character is not built in calm waters. It is built during storms. Ethics are not truly tested until doing the right thing costs you something.

That applies to individuals. That applies to families. That applies to companies.

Anyone can do the right thing when things are going their way. But when the walls are closing in, when the consequences of standing tall feel heavier than you can carry, that is when who you are shows up. That is when your values either hold the line or collapse under pressure.

I have seen people stand up and speak out even when it meant isolation. I have seen companies expose wrongdoing even when it hurts financially. I have seen families weather storms that would shatter most, choosing to heal rather than hide. That is real ethics. That is real strength.

But I have seen the opposite, too. People who lie, cheat, and manipulate their way to the top. Companies that bury the truth to protect profits. Families who smile for pictures and tear each other apart behind closed doors. Hypocrisy with a shine on it.

And I am not innocent. I have lied, stolen, sold drugs, cheated, and justified my behavior with some twisted sense of ethics. Even in addiction, even in the haze, there was a part of me that believed in something deeper. There was an inner compass pulling me back. I did not always live up to the standards I expected in others. That is hypocrisy at its finest. But I learned, and eventually I stopped repeating the same mistakes.

Maybe it is the Libra scales in me, obsessed with fairness. Maybe it is because I have seen injustice firsthand. Whatever the reason, I care about the truth. I care about transparency. I care about accountability, not from a desire for revenge but from a sense of justice. I believe what is done in the dark eventually comes to light. That is why I learned it is better to confess than to be caught. Better to live in the light than feed shadows.

I was not raised Catholic, but I understand the idea of confession now. There is something sacred about speaking your wrongs. Something freeing. It is a cleansing of the soul. I am grateful to be at a point where I do not have many secrets left. It is a lighter way to live, without skeletons rattling behind every door.

My mother has always been my confidante. She knows every one of my transgressions: the burglary, the drugs, the cheating. No one knows me better. I often confessed at the worst times, but I confessed nonetheless. In recovery, this is what taking a personal inventory is for. It is admitting to ourselves and to another human being the exact nature of our wrongs.

What breaks my heart is how rare integrity feels today. Everywhere you go, there is another scam, another snake, another person stepping on someone else to get ahead. Maybe I was a lawyer in a past life, not a defense attorney or a prosecutor, but someone who fought for justice. Someone who cared about truth, not just winning.

Our legal system is flawed. If you have money, you have options. If you do not, good luck. Public defenders are overwhelmed, and adequate representation is hard to get. I would almost rather represent myself. No one will ever fight for you like you will. And if you have the truth on your side, you already have the strongest argument in the room.

I still believe in America, not blindly but fully. This country has deep problems, but there is nowhere else I would rather be. Here, even if you are broke or broken, you still have a shot. You still have hope. You still have a path forward. That means something.

So, if you have skeletons, let them out. If you have secrets, speak them. Seek the light. Stand for something even when it costs you. Especially when it costs you. Ethics are not about being perfect. They are about being honest. In a world full of smoke and mirrors, the truth really will set you free. It shows who you are and who you are willing to become.

What type of person do you want to be?

"Labels are for filing. Labels are for clothing. Labels are not for people."—
Martina Navratilova

Labels

Gay. Straight. Mother. Father. Democrat. Republican. Felon. Christian. Muslim. Atheist. These are all labels. Labels help us by defining certain groups of people. They can describe a person's standing in society, political orientation, physical traits, or any shared characteristic.

Labels also hinder us by putting people in a box, reducing individuality to a single word. They shape opinions before we ever learn anything about the person behind the label.

When I was job seeking, having to explain my felon label was often insurmountable. I would walk into an interview, disclose that I was a felon, and immediately see their facial expression change. The conversation would shut down on the spot. I knew the interview was over.

That experience taught me how quickly one word can close a door. It showed me something deeper: labels, whether positive or negative, almost always flatten the truth of a person.

If you hear the word felon, what do you think with no context? Dangerous, immoral, selfish, manipulative. If you hear doctor, you probably think intelligent, caring, compassionate, trustworthy.

But what if that felon was convicted for shooting an intruder in a state without stand your ground laws? You might think protector or a victim of circumstance. What if they were convicted of a violent crime and later exonerated by DNA evidence? Your perception shifts again.

What if the doctor worked at a pill mill, handing out painkillers to anyone willing to pay? Suddenly, the positive label loses its shine. Instead of compassionate and trustworthy, you might think corrupt or predatory.

Even positive labels do not tell the whole story. Someone can be called a war hero or a genius, yet go home and abuse their family, cheat on their spouse, or numb themselves nightly. Brilliance or bravery does not make someone good. Labels can praise or condemn, but either way, they blind us to the complexity of the whole person.

The point is simple. We hear a label and jump to conclusions before getting to know the individual. We assume they fit into the same box as everyone else with that label. Labels can identify, but they should never define.

Being educated does not make someone wise. Having a criminal record does not make someone a second-class citizen. Having an addiction does not make someone weak. Undocumented does not mean criminal. Homeless does not mean irresponsible. Wealthy does not mean role model.

If we want to see people for who they are, we have to look past the shorthand and embrace complexity. Before we look up to someone or look down on them, we should learn who they are. Take labels with a grain of salt because they rarely tell the real story.

What label have you been given that you have had to outgrow?

"Sometimes you will never know the value of a moment until it becomes a memory."— Dr. Seuss

Memories

In the end, all we truly have are our memories. Stop creating them, and we stop living. I saw it in my father, my mother, and my grandfather. Their worlds gradually collapsed inward, life narrowing until memories replaced new experiences. Watching their lives shrink was a warning. Life will narrow on its own if you let it. The only way to resist is to keep creating, to keep living.

I watched my mother's depression cripple her, leaving her a shell of who she once was. She woke up disappointed to still be alive. She spent her days staring at the television, barely present, barely connected. She stayed in that purgatory for years, wanting more yet unable to summon the energy to change. Friends drifted away. Calls went unanswered. She constructed a box of loneliness and lived inside it. Misery became her comfort, painful yet familiar, easier than change. She drowned her desperation in liquor, never finding the peace she hoped for. Life became a loop. Day after day. Year after year.

But I also watched her start to rise. She switched medications and found one that finally helped. She still has difficult days, but her old self is beginning to shine through. I hear life in her voice again. Last week, she got back from her weekend in Galena, a trip she had skipped for years. She is reconnecting with friends, spending time with her granddaughters, calling my sister more often, and venturing back into the world.

I watched my father shrink in a different way. His world became incredibly small. The cycle was the same every day: the job he hated, the grocery store, Menards, home. Sometimes, three grocery trips in a day to stock up on cheap cuts of meat, condiments, and canned goods. He refused to go out to eat, even if someone else offered to pay. He would not go on vacation, attend a game, or go to the movies. His universe contracted until his closest companion was a tall Whiskey Sour.

With my grandfather, it was his health that collapsed his world. As his vision faded, so did his zest for life and eventually his will. His mind and body followed. He cycled in and out of nursing homes, regaining strength only to lose it again. He told us he woke up to blackness and wished he could end it. He said he lacked the courage to do it. His last years were brutal. A world of darkness, immobility, and nothing but thoughts and memories. It hurt to know those were the thoughts he lived in.

As his mind declined, he began confusing family members. He would sit in the living room mumbling to himself. If you asked him what he said, he became confused but tried to play it off. Eventually, he repeated my grandmother's name, "Anita," over and over, followed by "I love you," again and again.

And through it all, I saw the toll it took on my grandmother. For nearly five years, she was his caretaker. When he could walk, she took him on their daily routes through West Racine. When he grew weaker, all 98 pounds of her helped him into bed, into the car, onto the toilet, and into the bath. She visited him twice a day in the nursing home, every day, for hours each time. Her life was put on hold until he passed on Christmas Eve of 2014. She remained his partner, best friend, and devoted wife until the very end.

Yet she chose life. At 90, she still exercises, volunteers, travels, and leans on her faith. She continues to live despite tragedy and loss.

We all have dreams, weaknesses, and struggles. We all experience moments that shake our foundation and make us question everything. Megan always told me that happiness is a choice. We can crumble and mourn the rubble, or we can rebuild. The foundation may look different, but it can still be beautiful. We can look at yesterday with gratitude, appreciate today for what it is, and work toward the tomorrow we want.

I once heard that depression is holding onto what was, and anxiety is fearing what might be. Practicing acceptance allows us to keep living. Accept what has already happened. Have faith that things will unfold as they should. Stay anchored in the present.

At the end of our lives, all we have are our memories. So go live yours. Do the thing you have always wanted to do but never did because there was always an excuse. Be brave. Be fearless. Live your best life.

The last thing I want is to reach the end and realize I played it safe when I should have taken a chance. Life is not safe, and nothing is promised. Visualize what you want your life to look like and chase it, as if everything depends on it, because it does. The only limits we have are the ones we place on ourselves.

I have seen what happens when life shrinks to nothing but old habits, regrets, and fading memories. The antidote to becoming trapped in old memories is to make new ones. Bold ones. Lasting ones. Make memories worth holding. One day, they will be all you have.

"The eye sees only what the mind is prepared to comprehend."— Robertson Davies

Reality

Context Note:
This chapter explores how perception shapes reality. It touches on politics, history, and social bias. These are my reflections, not universal truths. You may disagree, and that is welcome. The goal is dialogue, not division. I share my view so we can all question what we believe and work toward better ways of seeing the world.

Beauty is in the eye of the beholder, and so is everything else. Our perception determines our reality. It shapes the meaning we assign to the world and to each other. The problem is that perception is not always accurate. It is based on how we receive and interpret information, and we rarely have the full picture. What we do have is filtered, biased, or incomplete. That makes our perception fallible.

We attach strongly to our viewpoints. We cling to our ideas as if being wrong diminishes who we are. This limits growth, problem-solving, collaboration, and healthy relationships. Many of us mistake being wrong with being unworthy. That belief alone can freeze our evolution.

Add confirmation bias, and things get even messier. If I believe the sky is green and two other people tell me they think the sky is green, my belief becomes stronger even if it is incorrect. Soon, I cannot even consider that the sky might be blue. There could be mountains of evidence to the contrary, and I still refuse to look. "The sky is green, and that is final." This is how outdated, harmful ideas survive for generations.

This same pattern fuels beliefs about race, gender, mental health, crime, addiction, and more. Closed mindedness, combined with a strong will, can be dangerous. Hitler drew power from unwavering conviction, charisma, and the ability to influence people who were lost, angry, or desperate for belonging.

Humans have a primal desire to belong. When we are insecure or searching for identity, we become vulnerable to manipulation. That is how people get pulled into white nationalism, extremist groups, anti-immigrant rhetoric, and other forms of hate. Not because the ideas are sound, but because the person delivering them offers certainty and belonging.

Be mindful of who you follow. Question what you believe. Stand for something real. The truth is inside you already. You just need to tune to the right frequency.

In today's climate, we must research for ourselves. With fake news, misinformation campaigns, biased media, fear-based messaging, and AI-generated videos, we cannot take everything at face value. We must learn to separate fact from fiction, strip away narrative, and gather information from multiple unbiased sources. Vet your sources. Examine motives. Become flexible in your thinking. Tune your perception like an instrument. Listen past the noise to find the truth.

It is okay to be wrong. It is okay to change your mind when new information arrives. Admitting you were incorrect does not lessen your value. If anything, it shows you are adaptable and capable of using logic and reflection to grow. It shows humility, which is rare and powerful.

Our perception is not reality. It is simply our interpretation of it based on what we know. If we learn more, our perception should change. If it does not, that speaks louder about us than about the world.

We must stop blindly following political parties, religious leaders, influencers, or loud voices delivering the wrong messages. Pretty lies can create devastating consequences.

We are meant to question. We are meant to analyze. Curiosity is who we are at our core. From atoms to galaxies, every advancement has come from challenging old ideas and embracing new ones. Our understanding grows when we release what no longer serves us.

Reality shifts when perception shifts. Stay open. Stay humble. Question everything. Learn. Grow. See the bigger picture. Keep your perception fluid and free of the beliefs that keep you small.

Transcend.

"Energy cannot be created or destroyed, only transferred."— *First Law of Thermodynamics*

Heaven and Hell

Context Note:
This chapter explores how perception shapes reality and touches on politics, science, and spirituality. These are my reflections, not universal truths. You may disagree, and that is completely fine. The goal is to open dialogue and explore ideas, not to impose absolutes.

I want to pose a theory on heaven and hell by blending theology with science. This theory is rooted heavily in energy, which I have referenced before, but I want to expand on it here.

The universe is made of matter and antimatter. Webster's dictionary defines antimatter as matter composed of antiparticles, and antiparticles as subatomic particles identical to other particles in mass but opposite in their electric and magnetic properties.

I believe human beings are conduits of energy, which many call the soul. Our bodies are vessels, and when they fail, the energy leaves. But what is the frequency of our energy?

People often say certain individuals carry magnetism, a gravitational pull that draws attention and influence. Think of figures like Jesus, Mohammed, Gandhi, Mother Teresa, or the Dalai Lama. On the opposite side, we have Hitler, Gaddafi, Charles Manson, Genghis Khan, and Saddam Hussein. Both groups altered history because of a powerful, energetic charge combined with the right moment in time.

Movements often arise when the collective consciousness aligns in a certain way. When a person with potent magnetism emerges at the right time, the world shifts. Like attracts like. Those with similar frequencies connect. Those with weaker energy can be pulled into a stronger force.

For the sake of theory, assume this is true. What does this have to do with heaven and hell?

When we die, our energy is released. The First Law of Thermodynamics states that energy cannot be created or destroyed; it can only be transferred. So where does that energy go? If like attracts like, and if energy moves toward similar frequencies, would our energy not be drawn toward a greater convergence of energy in the universe?

It seems vain to assume that the energy inside a human body is the strongest in the known or unknown universe. Would our newly freed energy not be pulled toward a larger energetic force somewhere in the ether?

My theory is that heaven and hell are not fixed places but convergences of positive and negative energy in the universe. They could be concentrated pockets of frequency rather than physical destinations. These pockets may shift like clouds in the sky. One cannot exist without the other.

Antimatter suggests that for every positively charged particle, there is a negatively charged counterpart. If the magnetic properties are opposite, then for every strong pull toward the good, there must be an equally strong pull toward the bad. This balance is essential. It is the yin and the yang. Light within dark, dark within light, the whole requiring both.

From this, many questions arise. Could this explain conscience? Is conscience the tension between two energetic forces, like magnets pulling at the same object? Do our actions influence the resonance of our energy and therefore determine what comes next? Could being born again simply mean that our internal energy has been realigned through healing, acceptance, and transformation?

Could heaven on earth be possible if humanity collectively aligned its energy, raised its frequency, and created a magnet strong enough to attract that positive convergence of energy toward us? Could the opposite also be true?

Maybe heaven and hell are not places at all but frequencies we tune into without realizing it.

I am not a theologian or an astrophysicist. What I am is someone who thinks deeply, uses logic, and is not afraid to question. I am not so attached to my former beliefs that I cannot explore new ones. For most of my life, I believed hell was nothing more than a fabrication designed to control behavior. Now, I am not so sure. I do not claim to have the answers. My goal is to encourage people to ask questions and to show that science and spirituality may intersect more than we think.

Perhaps the work being done at CERN, the particle collider in Switzerland, will bring us closer to understanding antimatter and, by extension, the metaphysical questions humanity has asked since the beginning. Maybe we will learn more about the universe and our place in it.

For now, all we have are our questions, our beliefs, and our energy.

"We are not human beings having a spiritual experience. We are spiritual beings having a human experience."— *Pierre Teilhard de Chardin*

God

I want to talk about my views on God. For a long time, even saying the word God left a bad taste in my mouth. It carried arrogance, frustration, and disbelief. Let me explain why.

I was raised in the Lutheran church. Sunday School, weekly services, Bible study, holidays, and Confirmation. I was baptized, had godparents, became a godparent myself, and was confirmed at sixteen. I knew the system well.

By high school, you could not tell me anything. I believed in something bigger than myself, but I was selfish. I did not believe in the stories of the Bible. Noah and the ark, walking on water, rising from the dead, burning bushes. I viewed the Bible as symbolic and moral, not literal. Someone once told me the word Bible stood for Basic Introduction for a Better Living Experience. I liked that.

The problem was that I had no peace. Not in my mind, not in my heart. I looked down on people who believed a higher being was personally guiding their lives. I thought it was vain to imagine a divine puppet master watching billions of people at once. Yet it also seemed vain to think we were the only intelligent life in the universe. I believed there was something beyond us, but not the God I grew up with.

It took a long time to understand that I get to define what God is to me. I'm able to develop a personal relationship with my Higher Power. Religious writings like the Bible, the Qur'an, and the Vedas are guidebooks, stories, and teachings meant to point us inward. They are meant to inspire us to seek, not to scare us into obedience.

Across nearly all religious traditions, the same messages appear. Love. Compassion. Strength. Responsibility. Taking care of ourselves in mind, body, and soul. Loving our neighbors. Praising God. Connecting to self, to others, and to something greater.

First is the connection to self. Self-care is often the first thing we neglect. Our bodies are vessels for the Spirit. Treat them well, and they carry us farther. Neglect them, and they break down sooner.

Next is the mind. We can challenge it, learn, grow, and keep our cognitive abilities sharp. Or we can numb it with endless screens and distraction. Mental illness is real, and getting help is nothing to be ashamed of. Asking for support takes far more courage than suffering in silence.

Then there is the spirit. When I neglect my spiritual health, my thoughts unravel, and my actions follow. Disconnection leads to disorder. I will talk more about spiritual health later, but for now, understand that this disconnection has consequences.

After connecting to ourselves, we connect to each other. Religion can be a beautiful force for this. It brings like-minded people together to seek guidance, build community, and work toward shared values. Churches, mosques, synagogues, and temples have done countless acts of good: feeding the hungry, sheltering those in need, helping families pay bills, cleaning parks, gardening, and supporting the vulnerable. These acts build connection and purpose.

But religion also has a darker side. Conflict arises when the connection breaks at any of the three levels: self, humanity, or God. The wars fought in the name of God did not come from divine intention. They came from pride, ego, misinterpretation, rigidity, and misguided passion.

Humans cling to beliefs. We reinforce them with confirmation bias. Once belief becomes identity, anything that challenges it becomes a threat. Debates turn to arguments, arguments to violence, violence to war. All supposedly in the name of God, but truly in the name of ego.

There are false leaders, too. Extremist groups. Manipulative cults. Abusive clergy. Mega church figures chasing money instead of service. Not everyone who claims to speak for God serves God. Some prey on the lost and the searching.

For anyone who has been misled or is unsure, I ask you to check your connection to your Higher Power. Meditate. Pray. Seek. The answers are within. We are not meant to follow blindly. We are meant to analyze and question, whether the influence comes from a religious leader, a teacher, or a politician.

It does not matter what religion you follow. Christian, Muslim, Jewish, Buddhist, Hindu, Agnostic, Atheist. We are all children of God in the sense that we all carry the same spark, the same inner light, the same capacity for connection. We all have the ability to heal and help others when we strengthen our connection to the Divine within us.

When we open our eyes to the interconnectedness of everything, the veil begins to fade. The Earth is alive, and we are part of it. We forget that we are spiritual beings having a human experience.

The sooner we stop taking life so seriously, the better off we will be. We have the universe within us, as Megan used to remind me. We are infinite beings in temporary bodies on a foreign planet woven with beauty and meaning.

Faith never had to be inherited. You get to define it. You get to shape your relationship with the Divine. When you open to it, you discover that God is not separate from you. God is the current of life itself. The signal runs through all things.

"When the doors of perception are cleansed, things will appear as they truly are. Infinite."— *Sir William Blake*

Lessons From Psychedelics

Hallucinogens have impacted my life and shaped my perspective in profound ways. Through them, I gained a deeper understanding of myself, how I relate to others, how I see the world, and my place in it. I learned lessons I am not sure I ever would have learned without those experiences.

People with little or no exposure to psychedelics often picture some burned-out hippie from the 1960s, aimless and fried. That stereotype is inaccurate. Psychedelics have been woven through human history for millennia. Ayahuasca tea is brewed by shamans in South America. Peyote is used by Native American medicine men. Morning glory seeds were used by the Aztecs for ritualistic and spiritual purposes. Those who took these substances were not dismissed. They were revered. Their journeys were considered sacred. They were seen as bridges between realms.

Many influential minds have also used psychedelics to expand perspective. Aldous Huxley explored mescaline and wrote The Doors of Perception. Francis Crick reportedly envisioned DNA's double helix while using LSD. The Beatles' experimentation reshaped modern music. Steve Jobs credited LSD with expanding his creativity. Ken Kesey's use influenced One Flew Over the Cuckoo's Nest. Psychedelics have shaped art, science, culture, and the way we understand consciousness.

Even the government experimented with LSD, attempting to use it as a truth serum. MDMA has been used in therapy to increase empathy, rebuild connection, and support healing. Hallucinogens have never been fringe. They have always been part of our story.

My experiences only confirmed what history already shows.

One night at Chris's house, after everyone else had gone to sleep, I stayed awake meditating. Around 4 a.m., I saw a white ball bouncing inside a square. Then the image zoomed out into a grid, each box with its own bouncing ball. The realization hit me instantly. The balls were people. The boxes were the emotional walls we built. The walls protect us from vulnerability, but they also keep us disconnected. The lesson stayed with me long after the mushrooms wore off. Race, religion, political affiliation, sexual orientation, none of it matters. We are all the same. Spiritual beings in human form. Beautifully different, yet the same. Keep the lesson. Toss the experience.

Another time, I took LSD with a woman I had been dating briefly. We went to Key Lime Cove, an indoor water park. Instead of having fun, everything looked fake. The whole park felt like an imitation of joy. The nearly five-hundred-dollar bill for one night felt hollow. I realized I would have preferred to have spent the time in nature.

Then I looked at the woman I was with. Our connection was shallow and rooted in a using lifestyle. As we walked up the stairs behind a tired father, lugging suitcases for his family, I saw myself in him. If I stayed with her, that would be my future. The path was right in front of me. I ended the relationship shortly after. I promised myself never to settle when choosing a partner. Not for loneliness or convenience. Only for genuine connection. Keep the lesson. Toss the experience.

Another time, Megan and I took mushrooms and went to Seven Bridges in Milwaukee. The world felt like a layered pop-up book. Families laughing. Children running. The forest alive. I felt like I could see reality's layers stacked like pages. I realized the world is a playground meant for exploration, wonder, and connection. Not domination.

When the park grew dark and the visitors left, squad cars suddenly pulled in, lights blaring. A moment of fear hit me. But after they passed, something shifted. I saw jail and prison differently. A long time out for adults. If you do not play by the rules, you do not get to play on the playground. It inspired something in me. I want people to be able to rejoin the playground. Too many people are stuck in time out, unable to live, unable to teach their children how to live. That needs to change. Keep the lesson. Toss the experience.

The most impactful psychedelic experience, other than confirming my belief in a higher power, was the one that motivated this book. It defined my goals and clarified my purpose. That story can be found at the end of A Vision of Hope: A Story of Redemption and Purpose.

Given everything that I have learned, I am all for psychedelics. If you are of sound mind, I encourage you to try them. They may help you work through something. They may help you find direction. They may help you learn to love yourself, accept yourself, and open your heart in ways you never expected. They can be life changing.

If you choose to explore psychedelics, I have suggestions:
• Be with people you trust
• Start small
• Do not force the experience
• Have someone experienced with you if it is your first time
• Avoid them entirely if you have schizophrenia, delusions, or difficulty distinguishing reality while sober

If you are scared, do not do it. Be mentally prepared. Remember, the experience always ends.

I have already made my stance on drug legalization clear. I feel the same about psychedelics. There are risks and benefits, but education and freedom of choice matter. I would not be the person I am today without several key psychedelic experiences.

They did not replace therapy. They did not replace healing or community. But they opened the door. They helped me discover myself. And sometimes, that is where real transformation begins.

Part III: Relationships, Responsibility, and the World Around You

Moves from the inner to the interpersonal and social world

"It is not the critic who counts... The credit belongs to the man who is actually in the arena."— Theodore Roosevelt

Competition

Competition can bring out both the best and the worst in people. At its healthiest, it pushes you to grow, break plateaus, and exceed your former limits. At its worst, it brings out ugliness. Athletes and fighters break the rules of their sport. People compromise their bodies for an edge. Politicians slander opponents. Wealthy families bribe schools and falsify records to secure their children's futures. All for the sake of winning.

In prison, competition is everywhere. You see poor sports, bad losers, and ungracious winners. The same people who pout and make excuses when they lose are often the ones who brag and boast when they win. I cannot do it. I am competitive by nature, and I have been athletic since childhood, but I refuse to let a win or loss hijack my peace of mind. If losing a game makes me angry, hostile, or upset, I will simply choose not to play.

Every week, they wheel a basketball hoop into the pod, and we play around the world. Sebastian and I have been teammates from day one. Joe, our cellie, switches partners, trying to beat us. He has succeeded once, and he made sure we heard about it. When he loses, though, there is always an excuse. When you are the top dog, you get a target on your back. For us, it is just something to do, a way to move our bodies and pass the time.

I will not let competition dictate my peace. I refuse to win and shove it in someone's face. That does not make you stronger. It makes you look ungracious. It shows you are not used to winning with maturity. A winner without a winning attitude is not worth celebrating.

Competition is about more than victory. It builds character, work ethic, resilience, dedication, teamwork, responsibility, accountability, and goal setting. If you gave everything you had and grew in the process, you should walk away proud regardless of the outcome.

The problem comes when we attach our worth to external results. Grades, promotions, admissions, achievements, praise. Our ranking in any system does not make us better or worse than anyone else. It only tells us how we compare in one category.

Our culture is obsessed with ranking everything. Talent shows. Game shows. Singing competitions. Leaderboards for anything imaginable. It becomes easy to lose perspective. Healthy competition is good. Letting the results define your value is not.

If you are going to compete with anyone, let it be the person you were yesterday.

"The mass of men lead lives of quiet desperation."— Henry David Thoreau

Complacency

So many of us fall into our lives instead of choosing them. One moment, we are young and dreaming. Then a series of events happens, and before we know it, thirty years have passed, and we are living a life we never intended. Some call it growing up. We set aside our dreams in the name of responsibility. We live for weekends, holidays, and vacations. If we are lucky, we enjoy a few years of decent health after retirement. We spend our lives waiting for the next event, killing time in between.

We find a job that becomes our career. Maybe it is not what we dreamed of as kids. Nobody grows up wanting to be a sanitation worker, a CNC operator, a roofer, or a janitor. But the pay is solid, the benefits are decent, and the company is stable.

It's really not that bad.

We meet someone. Maybe we have kids, maybe we do not. We get comfortable. We have had rough relationships in the past, and while the spark may be lacking, at least this person loves us. They are just as damaged as we are. And who wants to be alone? Maybe we once felt a deeper connection with Sarah or Susie, but this is fine.

It's really not that bad.

Together we build credit, get married, and buy a house. Two cars. A dog. A couple of kids. We save for their education. We work sixty hours a week, come home exhausted, down a drink, watch TV, and pass out. We repeat it the next day because that is what grown-ups do. Maybe the marriage is strained. Maybe communication is gone. But at least we are not like Al down the street paying alimony.

It's really not that bad.

Then the years fly by, and the questions start creeping in. Where did the time go? Is this really it? My job sucks. It is not that bad, but it sucks. The kids are grown, the house is quiet, and my partner and I have no idea how to connect now that our only role was being parents. Maybe this is what a midlife crisis is. This was not what I intended.

This is what I mean when I say our lives end up choosing us. We stay in jobs we dislike out of fear. Fear of instability, loss of security, or the unknown. We stay in relationships past their expiration dates for the same reasons. We settle because it is familiar. We trade potential happiness for comfort.

I do not want a life that is "not that bad." I do not want a life built around waiting for the next event. No one ever said settling was the best decision they made. This is not an excuse to quit when things get hard. Some things take work. But if you are deeply discontent in an area of your life, change it. Take control. If growing up means giving up on the life I want, then I will never grow up. I would rather chase my childish dreams than surrender to complacency.

If you are unhappy with your work, start moving toward something more meaningful. If you are stuck in a relationship that is going nowhere, free yourself before you miss a real connection while clinging to the wrong one. Life is too short not to make it your own. Find joy in the journey. Do not take life seriously, but take your life seriously.

Life is too short for "not that bad." Do not wait for a midlife crisis to wake you up. Choose now to chase what sets you on fire.

"We think we're separate because we have these bodies, but we're not. We are waves in the same ocean."— Thich Nhat Hanh

Interdependence

Something I like to tell people is that we are the sum of our past experiences. Everything we have felt, thought, and lived through shapes who we are today. It influences our actions, our worldview, and the decisions we make.

This is important to keep in mind because it helps us develop compassion and understanding, which are far too scarce in today's world. We condemn others for choices we disagree with, for opposing viewpoints, and for not conforming to what we believe is the right way of living.

If we remember that every person has experienced a different set of circumstances, we can begin to understand why they see the world the way they do. We can help each other heal. We can find ways to coexist.

The Bible says to Love Thy Neighbor. There are no conditions. It does not say Love Thy Neighbor if they look like you, vote like you, worship like you, or live like you. It simply says Love Thy Neighbor. Period.

Life wears us down. Trauma, heartbreak, disappointment, and stress can erode the compassion we once had. Our lens shifts. We harden. Sometimes it happens from personal experiences. Sometimes it is the influence of society. Living in a capitalist world where money and individual advancement often come before community does not help. Hatred can be taught. So can apathy.

Einstein once wrote: "A human being is part of the whole called by us Universe, a part limited to time and space. He experiences himself, his thoughts, and feelings as something separated from the rest, a kind of optical delusion of his consciousness. This delusion is a prison for us, restricting us to our personal desires and affection for a few persons nearest to us. Our task must be to free ourselves from this prison by widening our circle of compassion to embrace all living creatures and the whole of nature in its beauty."

Perhaps that is the truth we have been circling all along. Separation is an illusion.

We all need help at some point. We are social creatures. None of us is entirely independent. Whether it is rebuilding after a natural disaster, grieving a loved one, needing financial support, seeking guidance, or simply needing a friend to listen, we rely on others every single day.

In prison, the worst punishment is segregation. Being removed from killers, robbers, and rapists is not the punishment. The punishment is being removed from people entirely. Long-term isolation has been shown to affect in the brain the same way multiple concussions do. Some say this stems from ancient survival instincts, when being separated from the group meant danger from predators, the elements, or rival tribes.

Whatever the origin, the truth remains. We depend on one another for our well-being and our survival. They say a chain is only as strong as its weakest link. I say we strengthen the links. We lift others up so they can contribute to the whole with their full potential.

Let us celebrate our differences. Turk, an inmate here at Racine County Jail, told me something I liked. His relative once said, "Imagine buying a big box of crayons and a new coloring book. You open it, peel the wrapping off the crayons, and find that every single crayon is blue. You would get bored quickly." People are the same way. Our cultures, beliefs, and traditions bring color to life if we choose to see them that way.

Acceptance. Compassion. Understanding. These are the attributes we must practice if we are going to grow as a community, as a nation, and as a species.

It all begins with how we treat one another. I challenge you to treat the next person you meet as if they are family and see what unfolds.

"Too often we underestimate the power of a touch, a smile, a kind word, a listening ear... all of which have the potential to turn a life around."— Leo Buscaglia

Inclusiveness

In one of my journal entries, I wrote that I needed to be more aware of and inclusive toward people on the fringes. I believe this is something we all need to be better at as a society.

When I wrote that line, I could not help but think about school shooters. How many of them must have felt excluded, overlooked, or unimportant? How many cries for help went unnoticed? What if, instead of being in a treatment setting, the bullying Red Beard experienced had pushed him past his breaking point and toward violence?

Mass shootings are tragic on every level: for victims and their families, for the community, for the shame and grief carried by the perpetrator's loved ones, and for the perpetrator themselves, who are so damaged and alone that causing pain feels like the only way to be seen. They want to matter, even if it is in the worst possible way.

How many tragedies could have been prevented if just one person cared enough to reach out? A counselor. A teacher. A classmate. A co-worker. A neighbor. Anyone.

What if someone tried? What if someone noticed the quiet kid, the awkward one, the one who stood alone? What if they invited them to go bowling, or to a cookout, or simply took a moment each day to say hello and ask how they were doing? What if something that small could have changed their trajectory? What if kindness could have stopped Columbine, Sandy Hook, the Aurora theater shooting, or any of the countless mass murders we have seen?

What if more than one person tried? What if we smiled more? Checked in more. Listened more. Gave well wishes to strangers. What if multiple small acts of kindness, unconnected but consistent, prevented the next great tragedy?

What if we lived in a world less obsessed with ourselves and more aware of others? A world where we cared enough to notice when someone seemed off. Awareness is the first flap of the butterfly's wing.

I think back to my own life in shambles when I left treatment in 2018. I was going to Narcotics Anonymous meetings, desperate to stay clean, but feeling painfully alone. Then Melissa talked to me. She introduced me to her friends. She invited me to events. I remember standing outside the recovery club feeling awkward and anxious, unsure how to interact with anyone.

That simple act of kindness from a stranger made me feel accepted. It made me believe things could get better. Her inclusion played a key role in my recovery and may have been the difference between reclaiming my life and falling back into addiction, prison, or death.

All from one person taking the time to care.

We never know the impact we can have on someone. What seems small to us might be life-changing to them. A smile. A question. A moment of listening. A sign that someone sees them. It might be the moment they point to years later when asked, "What changed things for you?"

We never know what someone is struggling with. They could be on the edge without showing it. We live in a world where violence feels like a common language. It is in our shows, our games, our news. We cannot stop someone determined to cause harm, but we can make sure they know someone cares. That they are seen. That if they ever needed to talk, someone would listen. That they are loved. That they share the same inner light.

We can choose to care. We can choose to include. We can choose to notice those on the fringes.

And that choice might mean everything.

So today, I challenge you to be someone's Melissa.

"Surround yourself with only people who are going to lift you higher."—
Oprah Winfrey

Influences

I see so much talent go to waste behind bars. Artists, musicians, singers, rappers, athletes. And those are only the talents you can see. There are gifted minds here whose only audience wears prison scrubs.

This can be disheartening or inspiring, depending on your perspective. You can shake your head and think it is a shame that so much potential is going unused. You can feel disappointed that people with the skill to build a different life still ended up behind bars. Or you can see hope in the fact that many are paying for their mistakes yet still have something to offer. Some are using their time to sharpen their craft or develop a new one. With guidance, some could turn their talent into careers or at least have a positive outlet to carry with them on release.

Talent without opportunity often goes unnoticed. In the end, it is up to the individual to decide whether their passion becomes a pastime or a profession. We all reach moments where we question whether to chase our dreams or settle for something safer. Those are the moments when we need people who encourage us, who push us, who remind us that we can achieve.

As Will Smith said, surround yourself with people who "fan your flames." Surround yourself with people who encourage your passion rather than guide you toward the easy or conventional path. I know I do not want a conventional life. Life is not meant to be conventional.

For a long time, I surrounded myself with people who did not fan my flame. They did not challenge me to grow, and I lacked direction. I wandered from day to day without goals or purpose, a lemming headed nowhere.

It was easy. It was familiar. Nothing is challenging about staying the same. Growth is the tricky part.

Today, I try to surround myself with people who promote growth. People who make me examine my thoughts, beliefs, values, and actions. I do not want yes men. Sometimes being a good friend means telling someone what they do not want to hear. Hard truths can spark reflection and lead to meaningful change.

One of my old counselors used to say, "Hang out at a barber shop long enough, and you are sure to get a haircut." You are the company you keep. Peer influence is real. We all want acceptance and belonging, so we seek out people who act like us, think like us, and do what we do.

These connections can either lift us up or hold us back. Lack of diversity in workspaces, police forces, politics, or communities limits our understanding and prevents real solutions. Different perspectives matter.

In the county jail, we once had a deep conversation about personal accountability. I said we are all responsible for our actions and must own the consequences. I expected agreement. Instead, Polo, Mac, and to a lesser extent, Mo, disagreed. They argued their environment dictated their actions. They grew up in impoverished neighborhoods with limited options. From their view, surviving required selling drugs, carrying a pistol, joining gangs, scamming, or committing crimes to provide.

Then Dre spoke up about his cousin. He grew up in the same neighborhood, faced the same circumstances, and still chose a different path. He got good grades, went to college, found a good job, moved to a better area, avoided street life, and never went to jail. Same environment, different choices. Dre made the point better than I could.

Some people are born with every advantage. Others have to fight for a fraction of the same opportunity. That is the truth. Socio-economic conditions are unfair. Until the playing field is leveled enough for people to believe they can have a better life, we will keep having the same conversations.

Hope and positivity matter. We all hit moments when we do not feel motivated or optimistic. That is when the people around us must have our best interests in mind. Do they help us grow? Or do they keep us stuck?

Sometimes we outgrow the people we care about. Love does not automatically mean someone is good for us. Life changes, circumstances change, and we change.

I encourage everyone to examine their relationships. Look at who helps you grow and attach to them. Have meaningful conversations. Be open to different perspectives. And remember: if the people around you do not fan your flame, they will watch you burn.

"Power at its best is love implementing the demands of justice. Justice at its best is love correcting everything that stands against love."— Dr. Martin Luther King Jr.

Protect and Serve

Context Note:
This reflection looks at policing and justice in America. I write from personal experience, not from a textbook. These are my opinions based on what I have seen, lived, and researched. I know officers and their families may see things differently. That is okay. The point is not to attack but to ask how we can make law enforcement fairer, safer, and more trusted for everyone.

I believe the relationship between police and citizens needs an overhaul, especially in terms of mindset on both sides. Police officers are an essential part of society. I do not believe life would improve if we tried to police ourselves. But the polarization between officers and civilians is real. Too many murders at the hands of police go unpunished. Deadly force is used far too often, which is why body cameras have become necessary.

Bodycams are a step in the right direction. They show us an unbiased account of events, whether procedures were followed, whether force was justified, or whether misconduct occurred. They support transparency and accountability. They protect rights. They protect civilians. They even protect officers. Every officer in the field should wear one.

Bodycams also reveal the very real danger officers face. Shootouts, standoffs, and domestic disputes that escalate instantly. We see the ugly, like in the murders of Eric Garner, Michael Brown, and countless others. We also see the unpredictability and fear that officers experience every day. Understanding this matters. It teaches us how to act when interacting with police: remain calm, avoid seeming agitated, and speak with confidence and respect. It minimizes escalation.

With that said, people should understand that officers are not there to be your friend. They can legally lie to get you to incriminate yourself. They use psychological tactics to make suspects talk. My advice: say less, not more. Ask for a lawyer. Do not fall for the false sense of security when they say you are not under arrest "at this time." One wrong word can change everything. Ignorance of the law is not a defense, so learn the laws in the state where you live. High school should teach legal basics. Your ignorance will be used against you.

The tone of this relationship also needs to change. There is deep mistrust on both sides. Communities do not trust officers because of past abuses. Officers do not trust communities because of what they see and deal with every day. Civilians feel oppressed. Officers feel judged and unsafe. Both feelings are valid because, as I have said elsewhere, what we go through shapes our perspective.

So how do we fix it?

First, becoming a police officer should require a bachelor's degree. There is too much to learn to throw someone into the job with only months of training. Officers should be taught de-escalation, psychology, mental illness recognition, dispute resolution, and more.

Second, officers should undergo annual psychological evaluations. The job is mentally taxing. If an officer becomes jaded, biased, or unstable, they should not be in the field. That does not mean losing their job, but they should be moved somewhere less stressful. This protects them, their families, and the public. This should be in addition to a rigorous initial evaluation before being hired.

Third, accountability. Officers must be held to a higher standard. When they are not charged or receive a slap on the wrist for gross misconduct, the divide deepens. No one should be able to shoot a man in the back as he runs away, as in the case of Michael Slager, and avoid accountability.

Fourth, policing culture needs to change. It cannot be about covering for each other or hiding misconduct. Officers need moral fiber, the willingness to do the right thing even when it is hard. Especially when it is hard. That is the only way trust can be restored.

Fifth, we need to redefine what police departments are for. Their job is not to hunt for every minor infraction and make people pay. Even squad cars are designed to intimidate. Police should be peacekeepers, not soldiers. They should be trained to settle disputes, keep communities safe, respond to emergencies, and create a sense of security, not fear.

Officers should be part of the communities they serve. The divide widens when they feel above or apart from the people they are sworn to protect.

Looking globally, what we deal with here in the United States is not the norm. Most European countries train police as peacekeepers. Deadly force is rare and used only as a last resort. In the United Kingdom, most officers do not even carry guns. In Norway, training lasts three years and covers ethics, human rights, and psychology. Accountability is built into the system through external investigations and civilian oversight. Transparency is standard.

It does not have to be this way in America. Other countries have figured out how to police without fear, bias, or excessive violence. If we are serious about justice, safety, and improving trust, we need to learn from those models.

We need reform before we drift into a police state. This is why I do not enjoy shows like Cops, Live PD, Law and Order, NCIS, CSI, or Judge Judy. They reinforce a narrative that desperately needs to change.

Through unity and compassion, we can become better than we have been.

"Of all the forms of inequality, injustice in health is the most shocking and inhuman."— *Dr. Martin Luther King Jr.*

Tools We Deserve

Context Note:
In this entry, I talk about addiction treatment and drug policy. What I share is rooted in my own experience with recovery and my view of what works. I am not a doctor, scientist, or policymaker. I am one person who has lived it. These opinions are meant to start a conversation about solutions, not dismiss other approaches.

I want to talk about Ibogaine and Kratom, two substances that are illegal or restricted in the United States under the Controlled Substances Act. Ibogaine is Schedule I, classified as having no medical value. Kratom is legal in some states, illegal in others, and there have been attempts to make it federally Schedule I. Yet both have shown effectiveness in treating addiction, especially opiate addiction.

Ibogaine clinics exist in Peru and other countries. Ibogaine is made from a plant root brewed into tea and supervised by trained guides. It has shown remarkable success not just in treating addiction but in breaking it. Ibogaine is a hallucinogen. During treatment, participants often relive and work through past traumas, sometimes feeling as if they are communicating with deceased loved ones or confronting deeply buried emotions. It is believed that Ibogaine helps reset the brain's chemistry to a pre-addicted state. The experience lasts about a day but is physically, mentally, and emotionally exhausting, followed by several days of rest.

Kratom is a plant from Eastern Asia. It helps ease withdrawal symptoms: cramps, aches, anxiety, and insomnia. I have personal experience with Kratom. In 2016, while facing an alcohol and drug assessment for probation and unsure whether I would be tested, I stopped using and entered withdrawal. I drove to Illinois to buy Kratom legally, then committed a felony simply by crossing back into Wisconsin. Kratom brought my withdrawal symptoms from a seven to a three. It allowed me to function, work, and get through the day. A friend of mine who used heroin for nearly fifteen years got clean with Kratom as well. He did not get high from it, but he stayed stable long enough to stack nearly a year clean.

So why are Ibogaine and Kratom illegal or restricted? If they can help in what has been called the worst public health crisis of our time, why are they not available?

In my view, the answer is simple: money.

Kratom is inexpensive and grown overseas, meaning the United States cannot control the supply chain. Ibogaine grows in South America. Neither generates profit for pharmaceutical companies. And there is no money in curing addiction. There is enormous money in treating addiction indefinitely.

If Ibogaine cured addiction the way people claim, the pharmaceutical industry would lose profits from medication replacement therapies like methadone, Suboxone, and Zubsolv. They would lose profits from receptor-blocking drugs like Antabuse and Vivitrol. Replacement medications often cause dependence themselves, with withdrawals worse than the drugs they replace. Big Pharma becomes the legal drug dealer, and the revenue stream stays intact.

Here is a scenario that plays out more often than people realize.

Meet Johnny Addict.

Johnny gets hurt at work. His doctor prescribes Percocet, encouraged by pharmaceutical incentives Johnny knows nothing about. The pills work, but after a few refills, the doctor cuts him off. Johnny is hooked. He buys Percocet from friends, but his tolerance increases, his supply dries up, and the cost becomes impossible.

A friend introduces him to heroin. It feels like Percocet but stronger, longer lasting, and far cheaper. Soon, Johnny is using it not just to avoid being sick but to cope with stress, arguments, and daily life.

Johnny gets arrested for possession. Felony. He serves sixty days and probation. He tries to rebuild his life. He finds a job, gets housing, reconnects with his family, and tries to stay clean. But life piles on. His boss mistreats him. His car breaks down. He loses power one night and misses the bus, making him late. His boss suspends him without pay.

Johnny is overwhelmed. He wants relief. At the bus stop, his old dealer pulls up with a free sample.

Back to the races.

Johnny tries Suboxone, but it is expensive. He sells a few to afford the script, runs out early, and ends up back on heroin to avoid withdrawals. Jail again.

This time, he tries Vivitrol. It blocks the high, but not the feelings. He takes the shot for two months and stops.

Back to using.

Johnny wants to quit desperately. He reads about Ibogaine. He researches it. He wants to try it.

But he is a felon. He has no passport. He cannot leave the country.

He tries detox facilities, but he cannot afford them. They do not accept his insurance. The waitlists are long. He is stuck.

He tries to quit on his own.

He lasts one week.

Johnny dies of an overdose.

His wife becomes a widow. His son loses his father.

Johnny did not fail.

The system failed him.

The opiate epidemic is devastating and touches every demographic. Wisconsin passed Good Samaritan laws in 2017 to address overdose deaths, spurred by Senator John Nygren's personal experience with his daughter's addiction. When a problem hits home, urgency follows.

My stance is simple: use every tool available. Prevent future addictions through education. Treat addiction instead of incarcerating people. Allow the use of Kratom and Ibogaine. Let people choose the treatment that works for them. Cost should not decide who gets help. Politics should not either.

We deserve tools that actually give people a fighting chance.

"Elections belong to the people. It's their decision."— Abraham Lincoln

Politics: Will of the People

Context Note:
This reflection is political by nature. It is my perspective on how money and power shape elections, based on lived experience and study. I know some readers will disagree. That is okay. These thoughts are not meant as final answers, but as an invitation to dialogue. If we can disagree honestly and still work toward solutions, we all win.

Forgive me if I speak often about the law. My experience with the legal system has shaped my life, sharpened my beliefs, and revealed its inadequacies in painful ways. Combined with my core belief in free will and our constitutional right to life, liberty, and the pursuit of happiness, it is no surprise that I have strong opinions about our judicial system and our current political state.

Right now, I want to talk about something that dramatically impacts law, justice, policy, and daily American life: **money in politics.**

Money has corrupted the system. Here is why.

We first need to understand the obscene amount of money spent on elections in this country. Donald Trump raised thirty million dollars in the first quarter of his 2020 reelection campaign. If that were the quarterly average, that would be one hundred twenty million in a single election cycle before even considering his challengers. Bernie Sanders raised eighteen million. Elizabeth Warren raised twelve million. Kamala Harris raised six million. And they were only a handful of candidates.

This is just one race.

We have races for senators, members of Congress, House representatives, governors, mayors, judges, district attorneys, county clerks, aldermen, and so on. The Wisconsin Supreme Court race between Lisa Neubauer and Brian Hagedorn saw over forty-five million dollars in combined donations. That is for one justice out of five, each running every eight years.

What we have is a multibillion-dollar industry.

The people who shape laws that affect our lives depend on massive campaign contributions to obtain and maintain office. This does not come without consequences.

The first consequence is that running for office requires as much focus on fundraising as policymaking. Candidates cannot afford to alienate donors or stray far from party lines. If they do, they risk losing the financial backing that keeps them in office. They become torn between conscience and campaign viability.

The second consequence is the near impossibility of elections outside the Republican and Democratic parties. These are the only parties with enough resources and network power to run viable campaigns and gain recognition. Our founding fathers warned us against a two-party system. Yet the United States has become the poster child for it.

If you run as a third-party candidate, good luck. You will be out-funded, out-publicized, and largely ignored. If you run under one of the major parties, you must fall in line with the party's positions or face marginalization. You must please the donors or lose their support.

Imagine running for governor. Your views align more with Republicans, so you run as a Republican. You speak at debates and hold your own. Polls show strong support among moderates. Yet there is a problem. You oppose the border wall and take issue with ICE's approach. You support Medicare for All and believe healthcare should not bankrupt families.

The party warns you: **change your tune or lose our backing.** If you refuse, suddenly events get canceled, coverage dries up, and allies distance themselves. Maybe negative information surfaces. Maybe subtle threats appear. Either way, you are told to sacrifice your beliefs or sacrifice your political future.

Lose the race or lose your voice. That is the choice.

This system makes it nearly impossible for independent thinkers to serve the public. If both parties have preselected platforms, who decides what those platforms are?

The answer is simple.

Follow the money.

Candidates rely on donors to win elections. Donors hold the cards. If a candidate does not push the policies donors want, they are replaced by someone who will. This is not a democracy. It is influence disguised as representation.

Super PACs donate massive amounts of money anonymously. Corporations donate heavily to candidates who protect their financial interests. Lobbyists swarm Washington. Backroom deals are made. Favors are exchanged. Some politicians support bills in exchange for future jobs or benefits for family members. This happens more often than people want to believe.

Billionaires host fundraisers, form PACs, and influence candidates through donations. Look at the Koch brothers and Scott Walker. During Walker's campaign, a journalist pretended to be David Koch on the phone. Walker described his "divide and conquer" strategy openly. The news broke nationwide. Despite that, Walker survived a recall and served twelve years as governor. During his time, controversial bills were passed: allowing environmentally damaging fracking, reducing funding for public education while promoting charter schools, and refusing to issue a single pardon or visit a prison in a state with one of the highest incarceration rates in the country.

Democrats play the same game. This is not a partisan issue. It is systemic.

If Joe McPerson donates two hundred dollars to his preferred candidate, and Mr. Rockefeller donates four million through his businesses and PACs, whose voice does the senator value more? The answer is obvious.

That four million funds commercials, staff, events, travel, billboards, online ads, and speeches crafted to sway voters. Mr. Rockefeller's money buys visibility, recognition, and public opinion. Most voters do not research deeply. They respond to messaging crafted with money.

One informed voter is often drowned out by five misinformed voters shaped by marketing.

Thanks to Mr. Rockefeller, one vote becomes five.

So, what do we do about this?

We educate ourselves. We check facts. We examine sources rather than trusting news networks owned by the same billionaires funding candidates. We stop accepting vague promises without concrete plans. We demand specifics. We demand integrity.

We stop voting based solely on party. Too many people vote for all Democrats or all Republicans without regard for the individual. We hold elected officials accountable. If they betray the will of the people, they must go. Period.

We consider third- and fourth-party candidates. We open the door to new voices. Ideally, we eliminate party labels altogether. Candidates would be forced to stand on their own beliefs, values, and plans without hiding behind a party identity. More diversity in public office leads to more genuine dialogue and progress.

We must remove money from politics and restore the will of the people. Campaign finance reform is essential. No more Super PACs. No more unlimited donations. No more war chests. Enough is enough.

If companies and nonprofits are barred from donating, and individual contributions are capped at small amounts, campaigns will cost far less. We live in an age of social media, podcasts, livestreams, and online debates. We do not need billion-dollar campaigns. We need transparency, honesty, and accountability.

We must also restore trust in our voting process. The Mueller report confirmed Russian interference. If election results can be influenced, our entire system is at risk.

We can return to paper ballots. It would take longer, but it would be secure. We can have votes tallied by citizens, like jury duty. We can livestream the tallying process for transparency.

There are solutions if we choose to use them.

Imagine what we could do with the billions wasted on elections. We could fund universal education from pre-K through college. Combined with legalized drugs, we could afford universal healthcare. We could create a country where people trust politicians, where votes genuinely matter, where the sick get treatment without fear of bankruptcy, where police focus on real crime instead of punishing addiction, and where socioeconomic status no longer dictates quality of life.

Where the American Dream lives again.

This is America. This is the world I want to be part of.

Part IV: Vision, Purpose, and the Self

Focuses on personal evolution, expression, and reclaiming agency

"You'll never feel truly at home until you make peace with the person living inside you."— *Unknown*

Coming Home

To me, home is not where the heart is. It is not a physical location like your house or the city you grew up in. Home is a state of mind. It is a sense of comfort, the feeling of peace and security that comes when you can finally take down the masks and barriers you have spent your life building. That kind of home can only come from within. It is what people mean when they say being comfortable in your own skin.

I believe this only comes through self-reflection, exploration, and learning who you are: the good, the bad, and the ugly. It comes from understanding your strengths, weaknesses, goals, dreams, insecurities, traits, and characteristics. It comes from learning the essence of your identity. If we do not know who we are, how can we possibly feel at home within ourselves? How can we practice self-acceptance or learn to love ourselves? Instead, we end up searching for external solutions to internal problems.

For a long time, I had no idea who I was. My beliefs and values were handed down by family, friends, society, and expectations. I had no internal compass, and I was never comfortable. It did not matter if I was alone, with friends, with family, or in a crowd. I felt anxious and out of place. I tried to escape that discomfort with drugs and alcohol, exercise, music, gambling, sex, anything that would distract me from that gnawing emptiness inside. None of it fixed the wound underneath. It just covered it with a thin layer of distraction.

My first escape was drugs and alcohol. They numbed my insecurities, brought temporary peace, and made me feel a sense of relief that I came to depend on the way a diabetic depends on insulin. Without them, I felt lost.

In prison, I relied on gambling, exercise, and music to distract myself and pass the days. None of those things are bad on their own. They become a problem when they prevent growth. For me, they did. They kept me from looking honestly at my life, my patterns, and where I wanted to go.

During periods of sobriety, I used sex as an escape, sleeping with women I barely knew and being proud of it. It kept me from facing myself. It was only when I removed all these distractions that I began to learn who I was. Without that knowledge, I was a ticking time bomb, hurting myself and everyone around me.

Once self-love and acceptance take root, everything becomes easier. Acceptance of others, of our circumstances, and of life itself becomes second nature. We stop fearing rejection because rejection loses its power when we accept ourselves. Once that fear is lifted, the masks and walls come down. Our true selves emerge.

People who do not vibe with us naturally fall away, and there is space for real relationships. We communicate more openly and honestly. Our relationships become less codependent and more interdependent. We stop looking to others to supply peace because we already carry it within.

We become better role models for our children. We cannot teach them to respect themselves if we do not respect ourselves. But when we practice self-love, we can teach them confidence, kindness, empathy, and resilience.

We no longer depend on people, places, or circumstances to feel at ease. We can lose a job, mourn a loved one, face a breakup, relocate, or handle whatever life throws at us because we know who we are and trust that we will be all right. Our bonds grow stronger, both with ourselves and with others. We become comfortable in our skin. We discover new meaning for our lives.

Our boundaries expand. We become willing to take risks, to pursue what we want rather than take the easier, safer path. Excuses stop making sense. We know it is time to act and take ownership of our lives. We begin looking forward to the effort required. We begin imagining new possibilities. We know who we are and where we are going. Life regains purpose. We find peace, love, and serenity.

We finally find home.

"The two most important days in your life are the day you are born and the day you find out why."— Mark Twain

Purpose

I speak a lot about purpose. For a long time, I lived without vision or direction. I did not know what I wanted my life to look like or what I hoped to accomplish. My goals were superficial and selfish. I never planned for the future or considered how my decisions affected myself or others. I avoided responsibility, not knowing if I would be locked up or even live to see tomorrow.

The truth is, I had no idea what I wanted to do. I have always been competent enough to do anything I put my mind to. The problem was that I never put my mind to anything. I was too lazy, too complacent, and too unwilling to put in the work required to get anywhere. I was running on a hamster wheel.

For years, money was my motivation. It never fulfilled me. Money is simply a tool that allows us to live, to feel secure, and to pursue what matters. It buys comfort, experiences, and opportunity. But it can also blind us, becoming the pursuit itself rather than the means to pursue our purpose. Many of us start out wanting enough money to build a life. Somewhere along the line, the money becomes the mission.

At no funeral will you hear someone say, "Joe Blow made buckets of money, so he was a good man." No one cares how many vacations you took or what was in your bank account. What matters is the caliber of your character and the essence of your spirit.

Still, we all need money to survive. So, we work jobs to pay the bills. Yet how many of us dislike where we work, who we work with, or what we do, but stay out of obligation, fear, routine, or comfort? Too many people live lives they are dissatisfied with, but remain anyway. Thoreau wrote, "The mass of men lead lives of quiet desperation." I saw that everywhere, and I lived it too.

When we go against our nature, when we abandon what we were meant to do, we remain discontented. A life of purpose is a life well lived. My father worked a job he hated for decades. It drained him. I promised myself that would never be me.

For years, I heard people tell me I had potential. Potential is unrealized talent. Everyone has it in some form. We all have a skill, that thing we do where everything feels aligned. Find your thing. Tap your potential. Live your life on purpose.

The real work is taking the risk. It is discovering what fuels your inner spark, what fans your flames, and then running with it. What makes your light shine brighter when you do it. That is what you should devote your time and life to.

I will end this with a suggestion. Never stop dreaming big. Never let anyone tell you something cannot be done. Whether you believe them or believe in yourself, you are right.

What is the thing you would do even if you were not paid?

"Hope is being able to see that there is light despite all of the darkness."—
Desmond Tutu

Hope

For me, hope meant believing I could change when everything in my past told me I could not. It meant believing a better, more fulfilling life was possible.

There is nothing sadder than the death of hope. Hope is the wellspring that allows us to persevere. Hope is the belief that things can improve. Hope is what carries us through the bleakest circumstances. You cannot have faith without first having hope.

The problem is that sometimes we look for hope in the wrong places. We get lonely and think dating sites will cure that emptiness. We feel trapped in a dead-end job and hope some employer will stumble across our resume and rescue us. Or we move to a new city, thinking the new scenery will erase the pain of the old one.

But hope must start from within. We need to learn to soothe our loneliness, whether someone is in our lives or not. We need to use our dissatisfaction with a dead-end job to ignite a new path instead of drifting into the next Monster or Indeed posting. And moving to a new city can be part of growth, but not an escape. We carry our baggage wherever we go unless we open it and deal with what is inside.

The other day at MSDF, we watched What Doesn't Kill You with Ethan Hawke and Mark Ruffalo. Hawke plays Paulie. Ruffalo plays Brian. Two lifelong friends, raised in the same environment, pulled into the same crime world. After serving prison time, they face different paths. Brian tries to rebuild his life, repair his marriage, and be present for his sons. He slips, but he keeps trying. Paulie wants the armored truck heist they always dreamed about. He believes that one big job is his ticket to a better life. Brian turns him down. Paulie does it anyway. Brian stays free. Paulie gets fifty years.

The difference between them, as I saw it, was hope. Paulie put all his hope in money. Brian put his hope in family and redemption. Same starting point. Same environment. Same obstacles. Different sources of hope. Different ending.

Whether in our own lives, in the lives of people around us, or in stories told on screen, the same truth appears: hope shapes the outcome.

No matter how painful, irreversible, or impossible your situation feels, hold on to hope. Life changes. Circumstances evolve. Even in the darkest places, possibility exists. Imagine being in a concentration camp during the final days of World War II. Death must have felt certain. They could not have known liberation was imminent. Some lost hope and gave up, perhaps speeding their own suffering. Those who held on, even without certainty, lived to see the impossible become real.

Hope is like a baby faith. Hope believes that things can work out. Faith knows they will. What we put our hope and faith in determines everything.

Hope is the seed.

Faith is the root.

And the current that carries us forward is already flowing through us, connecting us in ways we may not yet fully understand.

"You don't have to be great to start, but you have to start to be great."— Zig Ziglar

Taking Action

For a long time, I failed to act in many areas of my life. I did not seek help when addiction was destroying me. I did not try to make a difference in my community. I did not take steps to build the life I wanted. I put off what I could do today for tomorrow, and tomorrow never came.

Often, especially in active addiction, we picture what we are going to do with our lives. We imagine business ventures, inventions, creative pursuits, grand plans for the future, and the impact we want to make. But ideas without action are just fantasies.

I can remember some of the visions I had while intoxicated. Magnum Electronics, the audio company Christoff and I were going to start, specializing in systems for golf carts, ATVs, and marine vehicles. Or the marketing campaign I created for SoBe. I even wrote to Pepsi and offered to put the pitch together at my own expense, but when they said they did not accept outside marketing, the idea died. I came up with a slogan for Mountain Dew, complete with an ad campaign. None of these ideas became reality because I never followed through.

I learned the hard way that ideas die when action is absent. Action is the only thing that matters.

There were several reasons these ideas declined. The first was a lack of passion. If I do not truly care about something, I will not go out of my way to make it happen. Passion is the spark that brings an idea to life.

If passion is present, the next step is research. With Magnum Electronics, I had only a basic understanding of car audio, circuitry, and wiring. I would have needed to study, learn, and sacrifice to bring the idea into existence. Real action requires dedication, consistency, and a belief strong enough to keep going when the excitement fades.

After research comes planning. How will I implement my idea? What steps do I take? Do I need a business plan? Should I write it or hire someone? Do I need funding or investors? What does the entire process look like from start to finish?

Then comes implementation. Many ideas die at this stage. A decision without action is just a thought. I could decide to start a business, join a charity, or explore a new spiritual path, but if I never take the next step, nothing happens.

This was a difficult lesson for me. I was a master procrastinator well into adulthood. I wanted results without working for them. Life does not work that way. If I want to lose weight, I cannot go to the gym and watch other people work. If I want to get clean, I cannot go to one meeting and expect a miracle. If I want a new job, I cannot sit around waiting for one to fall into my lap. It takes initiative.

Being a doer takes practice. It takes effort. It is easy to put off what feels uncomfortable or overwhelming. But once we push ourselves to act, we start reaping benefits. The pride and sense of accomplishment that follow are powerful motivators. Seeing the fruits of our labor pushes us to take more action.

The lesson is simple, but it took me far too long to learn. If we want a better life, we need to identify what we want, prepare for it, and then do the work. Discover what matters to you, what you are passionate about, and what direction you want your life to take. Set goals. Create purpose. Give yourself a reason to get out of bed. Stop treading water and start swimming toward something.

Once you know your direction, you need faith, belief, and conviction. Then you walk your path fearlessly. This does not mean ignoring others' advice, but it does mean not letting other people's doubts derail your purpose. Change feels uncomfortable, but discomfort is growth. I would rather switch paths a thousand times while learning than stay stuck on the easy route that leads nowhere.

The saddest life is one unfulfilled. Identify where you want to go and who you want to be. Plan how to turn that vision into reality. Then take massive action. Dedicate yourself to creating the life you dream about. Imperfect action is better than no action. Even one step can shift everything.

You figure it out as you go, but you must keep moving. Let the fire inside you fuel your journey. Find what you love. Work toward it like your life depends on it. Because if you want a life worth living, it does.

You do not build a life by thinking about it. You build it one bold step at a time.

"Music is what feelings sound like."— Anonymous

The Sound of Survival

Music saved me. It carried me through my worst times. Expression through sound was my first passion, the first thing that made me feel connected to something larger than myself.

From a young age, I have been an aficionado. Stephanie gave me my first cassette, the band Live!, when I was three. My second was No Mercy. In elementary school, I had my first performance singing "You Were Meant for Me" by LeAnn Rimes. My first concert was the Backstreet Boys at eight. I discovered rap when I heard the Slim Shady LP in fourth grade. I began writing music at sixteen, immersed myself in it at twenty-two, recorded my first song after my first prison stint at twenty-four, and had my first performance outside jail at twenty-six. The firsts go on and on.

When I was little, Stephanie babysat me. She would put me in a recliner, crank the stereo, and let me rock back and forth until I fell asleep. The music drowned out everything else. Even then, I did not realize it, but that was the first time my mind was ever quiet. It was the first time the noise inside me faded, like finding the right frequency.

Music spoke to me. It made me feel. The phonetics, the way sound hits the ear. With rap, it was a puzzle. How to create rhyme patterns in different ways while conveying meaning. I was always a gifted writer. My mother and sister wrote as well, so maybe it was in my blood. In high school, two of my poems were selected for publication. I was a writer first, then taught myself how to apply that skill to music.

During my first time in prison, I wrote constantly. They say it takes ten thousand hours to master something. I put in the hours. I would stand in the corner of my cell, one finger in my ear, rapping into the wall to hear how my voice sounded, since I had no studio. I worked on delivery. I wrote and wrote and wrote. Sometimes, until three or four in the morning, I would listen to the radio and ignore the lyrics so I could write my own versions over the beats.

I analyzed everything I heard. The engineering, the sound effects, voice effects, ad-libs, and delivery styles. I studied Andre 3000's ability to use half a word to complete a rhyme and start the next line. I dissected Eminem's rhyme schemes, his alliteration, how he packed consonants and vowels together, and how he fit multiple rhymes into tight spaces. I admired Lil Wayne's metaphors, double meanings, flips of phrases, and wit. His punchlines made me rewind because I missed the next bar. I loved Rae Sremmurd's energy, their distinct sound, and how their delivery could lift my mood instantly. I loved The Game and Young Jeezy for attitude, 2 Chainz for punchlines, and Big Sean for his delivery. I took the parts I loved from each artist and blended them until I found something uniquely mine.

In prison, I had no beat to dictate what I wrote. Inspiration came however it came. Sometimes a topic. Sometimes a title. Sometimes one phrase sparked a verse. Then a hook. Then another verse. Before I knew it, I had a song.

In the free world, I worked with producers who built beats from scratch. I would sit with them as they layered sounds until the beat took shape. The beat set the tone. It told me the subject. It gave me the feeling. Whether I watched it being created or heard it finished, it guided the direction of the song.

Then came the engineering process. Recording raw vocals, layering takes, adding ad-libs, and choosing the right effects. Getting it just right. There is nothing like the moment when the track is finished, the speakers blasting, and you smile because you created something from nothing.

Performing is the cherry on top. Sharing your work, your voice, your story. When people feel it, when they relate, when they say they mess with it, you know you touched something real. I wrote to survive, but when others connected, it meant I was not alone.

Music was my first passion. When I was in the creative process, I felt peace, connection, and purpose. While music is no longer the center of my life, it helped me persevere. It gave me an outlet. It became part of my platform. It will always be an essential part of my identity.

When I had nothing else, I had a beat and a pen. And that was enough to keep me alive.

Part V: Universal Truths and the Bigger Picture

Brings it all home — shared humanity, possibility, and time

"Somewhere, something incredible is waiting to be known."— *Carl Sagan*

Life Beyond Earth and Our Human Potential

Context Note:
This essay mixes science, spirituality, and social critique. I do not pretend to have all the answers. These are my thoughts, questions, and ideas about where humanity could go. Some readers will see things differently, and that is perfectly fine. The purpose is to stretch our imagination, not to declare doctrine.

I think it would be incredibly vain to believe that we humans are the only, or the most intelligent, life form in the universe. We know next to nothing about how the universe works. We do not know how big it is, we do not fully understand antimatter, we do not know what is on the other side of a black hole, we do not understand the possibility of wormholes, and we do not yet grasp the nature or shape of time and space. We have far more questions than answers.

Our knowledge has expanded rapidly since the 1980s with the rise of computer power, and I expect breakthroughs to continue at a fast pace despite attempts to slow progress through restrictions on research and a social focus on money over science. That is a conversation for another day. The point is that we still know relatively little.

Believing that there are no other intelligent (or more intelligent) life forms in the universe is adopting a very narrow view. Just because we are unaware, assuming we truly are unaware, does not make something untrue. It simply makes us ignorant of what is true.

There are many reasons people cling to disbelief. Religion is one. The Bible says man was made in the image of God, but it does not say that other intelligent beings were not created. It does not say that humans are the only design. If you believe in angels or demons, that alone is a belief in non-human intelligences. Could the word alien simply be another name for what past cultures described as angels or demons? Could all three exist?

Others resist scientific advancement out of fear. They say we should not "play God." But if we are created in God's image, would He not want us to grow into the best, most advanced version of ourselves? Would He not want us to use the analytical, curious minds He gave us? If we are His children, would He not want us to evolve, learn, and seek truth?

Fear is often the real reason. Fear of challenging old beliefs. Fear of upsetting the familiar. Fear of a God who punishes instead of a God who loves. I do not believe in a jealous, vindictive God. I believe we were meant to think, question, explore, and grow.

Humanity has always believed things that later proved false. That does not make us foolish. It means we learned. It means we evolved. We were not meant to follow blindly.

I believe spirituality and science intersect at a point we have not yet reached. If we keep connecting the dots, the picture will become clearer. I hope that one day people realize that being pro-science is not the same as being anti-God. My Higher Power guides my life, and I believe that ten, one hundred, or one thousand years from now, scientific breakthroughs will reveal truths about God, the soul, the afterlife, and the forces that shape existence. Awareness brings life.

Another reason for disbelief in other life forms is the idea that "I need to see it to believe it." That mindset is easy to challenge. We cannot see air, germs, ultraviolet rays, radiation, gravity, carbon monoxide, or the particles that make up light. Yet we believe in them. There are countless things we have not seen with our own eyes that undeniably exist.

I have never seen a terrorist, a tornado, an Eskimo, or a wildfire with my own eyes, but I do not doubt their existence. Closed-mindedness gets us nowhere. I take the information available, apply my belief system, use logic and reason, and come to conclusions.

I believe exploring the cosmos is our higher calling. Humans are explorers. We migrated out of Africa and settled across the world. We explored oceans, jungles, deserts, and every inhospitable environment. Our desire to push boundaries did not end. We want to understand why things happen and how the universe works. We search for synchronicity and connection.

Space is our next frontier. First our galaxy, then others. It is what we are meant to do. We are meant to settle on other planets, encounter what exists, and seek out what lies beyond. Human beings are creators, builders, adventurers, philosophers, healers, inventors, motivators, visionaries, and problem solvers. Everything that exists began as a thought. Thoughts change the world.

From the inventors and scientists who solved the problems of their age, such as Edison, Tesla, and Franklin, to leaders who pushed for moral evolution, like Martin Luther King Jr., Kennedy, and Gandhi, to the minds who studied the human brain, like Freud, Jung, and Cajal, to the people who challenged oppression and pushed humanity forward like Washington, Lincoln, and Moses, we see the same pattern. One spark comes from an individual, but it is the masses who carry the flame.

Only through unity can we find a collective purpose. If we set aside our political, religious, and cultural differences, we can move together. If we stop choosing leaders driven by greed, hate, and division, we can rise. There are no disposable human beings. Everyone has something to contribute. We need leaders who uplift, inspire, and empower.

Time is not on our side. First, we need to save our planet. We need to take back our government from special interests and corporations. We need to stop enabling oppressive regimes. We need accountability, transparency, and integrity at every level. We need a shift in values. We need to be better and do better.

How can we explore the universe when we cannot manage ourselves on Earth? Greed grips the world. Those with everything control the many who have little. Most people are given just enough to stay content, but not enough to be free. Fear is used as a tool. Violence dominates headlines. Catastrophe is always around the corner.

God's plan for us is to come together.

To do that, we must remove corrupt leaders and manipulative power structures. We must replace them with people of integrity and intention. If we cannot trust our leaders or their motives, we need new ones.

Once we regain control, we can build systems that help people contribute rather than struggle. We can shift away from a capitalist model that rewards greed and punishes the vulnerable. We can focus on science, unity, compassion, and the advancement of humanity as a whole.

We can build a society rooted in interdependence, understanding, and the search for truth. We can deepen our connection to ourselves, each other, the earth, and God, however each of us understands that word.

The only limits we have are the limits we place on ourselves. That is the veil we were born under, the illusion we inherited.

The stars are not the limit. Our mindset is.

"Our ability to reach unity in diversity will be the beauty and the test of our civilization."— Mahatma Gandhi

The Language of the Gods

It is crucial that we embrace our individuality. Not just accept it, but cherish the things that make us different. Our cultures, our appearance, how we speak, what we think, what we believe, our morals, our food, our shared and diverse histories. The world is one giant melting pot, and we are better because of it.

I pity those who build their identity around disliking others for their differences. Not only because of the arrogance and vanity of that mindset, but because their world becomes so small. Closed-mindedness limits experience, connection, growth, and understanding.

I do not want to live in a world where everyone looks, acts, and thinks like me. Without friction, there is no growth. If I surround myself only with people who think as I do, my perspective never gets challenged. My beliefs never evolve. I stay locked in the same thoughts and behaviors because that is all I see reflected around me.

I spoke earlier about diversity and shared the crayon analogy. If we learn to love our own shade, we can appreciate the hue of others far more easily.

Loving ourselves, fully and honestly, is the core of it. Learning not to hide parts of ourselves depending on who is around us. If you feel the need to hide who you are, change your surroundings, not yourself.

Being bold and fearless in our identity is real courage. The devout who stay devout among non-believers. The gay man or woman who refuses to shrink. The Black man who remains proud around people who might belittle him. A person is a person. Every one of us deserves equal respect, no matter our differences.

It is heartbreaking how much insecurity still exists in this world. How are we still dealing with racism? How are people still not accepted for who they love? How do we still have massive divides between the world's major religions?

We do not choose our hair color, eye color, skin color, height, mental or physical abilities, or disabilities. Our DNA is not self-selected. To dislike someone for traits they had no control over is cruel, misguided, and reflects more about the person casting judgment than the person receiving it.

To dislike someone for their sexuality is equally absurd. We do not choose who we love. For me, I could not choose to be attracted to a man because that is not who I am. But who am I to judge someone whose orientation is different. Their life does not affect mine. It is not my place to tell anyone who to be or how to live.

Some argue from religious grounds, but not everyone shares the same belief system. That is okay. If there are consequences in the afterlife for following your heart, that is between the person and their Higher Power. Live and let live.

You cannot force someone to believe what you believe. Conviction comes from within, like a quiet voice beneath the noise. If a belief strengthens your life, aligns you with your values, helps you connect with others, and makes you more compassionate, I support it.

We all need to grow up. Stop worrying about the next man and look inward. Understand who we are. Decide what we believe. Find our direction, our purpose, and our sense of self-love. When we turn inward, we spend less energy judging outward.

Once we have inner peace and self-acceptance, we can help others do the same. The world does not need to be full of hate. It is not about convincing others to believe what we believe. What works for me may not work for someone else. What matters is becoming aligned with our Individual Truth and Inner Light. We can guide others through our example, but the journey is personal.

This is what religion is supposed to be. Helping people discover their path, deepen their connection to their Higher Power, and unlock their inner divinity without imposing a belief system.

Once we embrace who we are, we can embrace others as they are. It all comes down to connection: with ourselves, with each other, and with our Higher Power.

It is about filling our hearts with love, because Love is the Language of the Gods. Love conquers all.

In the end, Love always wins.

"You can't change the past, but you can rob the future by wasting the prese nt."— Anonymous

Time

As I mentioned before, I try not to waste my time in here. I have spent too many years behind bars doing things that added nothing to my growth. I played cards for Zu Zu's and Wham Wham's, read books that were entertaining but did nothing to develop me, watched mindless television, and took part in conversations that were destructive instead of constructive. I try not to live that way anymore. I make use of whatever time I have, no matter where I am physically.

Time is the only commodity we can never replace. Money, power, prestige, jobs, love, and even health can sometimes return after loss. But time never does. Once time is gone, it is gone.

The concept of time trips me out. Einstein said time is relative, and he was right. Time is just a measurement of how long it takes our planet to complete a lap around a giant fireball in space. That measurement changes depending on distance. A year on Saturn is not a year on Earth. A year on Neptune is something else entirely. What happens when you go beyond orbit altogether, where you are no longer circling anything? Does time cease to exist without an orbital reference point? Is time just a construct of our minds, like inches or liters? If so, time travel could be possible, like moving forward or backward along a ruler. And what happens to aging as we travel deeper into space, where time moves more slowly? Maybe time is a veil, thin in some places and dense in others. Maybe aging is just the cumulative effect of gravity pulling on our bodies, breaking us down. Time is strange. It fascinates me.

Or maybe time is simply one layer of reality among many. Some believe the ancient pyramids were energy transmitters, sending and receiving frequencies, and that time travel might have been possible inside them. We may never know.

What I do know is that time is finite, and I do not want to waste any of what I have left. We are remembered by the impact we leave on the people around us, on our communities, and on society as a whole. The memory of who we were and what we did with our time here is what lives on.

I do not want my legacy to be that of a man who never lived up to his potential, who lacked the confidence to aim higher, who spent most of his life caught in addiction and incarceration. That is not a life of impact.

I do not want a life I merely "get through." Too many people wake up simply wanting to survive the day. That is one of the saddest things to me. A life without purpose. Do not count time. Make time count. Find your purpose, use your time, and live for today.

I know I will.

Closing Thoughts

If the memoir showed the storm, these reflections were written in the quiet moments between the lightning. They were my way of processing what I was going through, of making meaning out of the mess, of slowing down long enough to hear myself think.

If you are ready to put these reflections into practice, turn to the workbook.

If you have made it this far, I hope something here stayed with you.

I hope something challenged you.

Or softened you.

Or reminded you that healing is not a destination. It is a conversation. Ongoing. Unpredictable. Necessary.

So keep writing.

Keep asking the hard questions.

Keep choosing to stay awake to your own life.

And if you find yourself lost again, remember this: the Light has always been inside you.

This is your vision now, too.

You have already come this far.

You have already lived a vision of hope.

Author Note

Thank you for spending time with these reflections.

I did not write them to sound wise or polished. I wrote them because I needed to process what I was going through. Most were scribbled in a jail cell or in the treatment program that followed. Others came during recovery. Each one came from a moment that asked me to slow down, to look inward, and to keep going.

In writing these, I was not just healing. I was hoping. Hoping they would one day help someone like you.

If this collection has stirred something in you, whether clarity, discomfort, or curiosity, I hope you will take the next step.

I have created a companion workbook to go alongside A Vision of Hope: Reflections. It includes:

• Guided prompts
• Journal space
• Exercises and questions
• Tools for reflection, healing, and growth

Whether you are walking through addiction, loss, trauma, or simply trying to reconnect with yourself, the workbook is designed to meet you where you are and help you build from there.

You can find it online or request it at your local program, school, or library.

This journey is not linear. But it is yours. And I am grateful to walk a few steps of it with you.

— Andrew Drasen

About the Author

Andrew Drasen writes at the intersection of recovery, purpose, and reform. His trilogy — A Story of Redemption and Purpose (memoir), Reflections (principles), and the Workbook (practice) — forms a complete path from story to perspective to action. His life was reshaped by addiction, incarceration, and ultimately by the 2025 death by suicide of his fiancée, Caroline. That loss ignited a commitment to reach people before the cliff's edge and to change the systems that push them there.

Reflections distills the lived experience of the memoir into clear, usable principles you can apply now, then deepen through the companion Workbook. Together, these books anchor the A Vision of Hope Treatment Curriculum, designed for programs, reentry settings, groups, and individuals. An A Vision of Hope Skool community is launching to extend the work through aftercare support, a virtual IOP style option, and a structured community for anyone ready to heal with others.

Pair with:

• *A Vision of Hope: A Story of Redemption and Purpose* — the narrative that gives the principles weight

• *A Vision of Hope: The Workbook* — the tools that make the principles stick

Andrew's purpose goes beyond the page: to help people heal and to drive meaningful reform in recovery, reentry, and mental health, so dignity and outcomes improve in the real world.

Connect:

andrew@avisionofhopebook.com • (262) 383 1761 • avisionofhopebook.com

www.ingramcontent.com/pod-product-compliance
Lightning Source LLC
Chambersburg PA
CBHW031218120626
46545CB00003B/901